CW00641138

Black Bullets
in the Sweet Jar

Alison Carr

Black Bullets
in the Sweet Jar

Alison Carr

Smokestack Books
1 Lake Terrace,
Grewelthorpe,
Ripon HG4 3BU

e-mail: info@smokestack-books.co.uk

www.smokestack-books.co.uk

Text copyright 2023,
Alison Carr,
all rights reserved.

ISBN 9781739173036
Smokestack Books
is represented
by Inpress Ltd

Contents

Arrival

Pebbles bounce on the shell of my mind
Like gravel stirring my concrete thoughts.

I try hard not to let others panic,
Play it down:
The silver knife, the cut brain.

The professor arrives,
Antiseptic gloves,
Metal instruments on a tray.

He cuts into my shaved head.
Meatloaf is playing somewhere.

Thick fingers fiddle with brain tissue,
Blood mesh.

His bear-like hands
Sieve through my mind.

Play Away

Jackanory-story books curl their pages,
The child climbs the ladder into darkness,
Dandy, Beano, Twinkle,
Snakes and Ladders, Twister,
Pandora has let the hissing serpent of jealousy
Out of the dressy-up box.

Life joins hands with Florence and Zebedee,
Parsley speaks,
Professor Yaffle yawns,
Handprints on the wallpaper,
Lego walls crumble,
Black-board chalk screams.

Abacus, building blocks,
One, two, three coloured bricks,
Turning the page
Speech-bubbles,
Swirling colours,
Comic characters,
Kaleidoscope of hurt and disappointment.

Thundercats roar at the gates of Castle Greyskull,
Rapunzel spins, spins her beautiful hair,
Fantasy's ache grows thin,
Magic roundabouts whirl,
Seasons turn,
The fieldmice scamper,
Hickory-dickory dock.
Hamble stares out of the arched window.

Tiddlywinks, Scalextric,
The magician's sleight of hand,
Punch touches his jester's cap;
That's how you do it.
Captain Hook is still searching for Peter Pan.

The Old House of Childhood

Everything was so big,
I lived in the soft pages
Of fairy-tale books.

Gobstopper Days

Bulls' eyes in the sweet-shop window,
A toffee sweet haze
Of penny dips, licked fingers,
Sugar sprinkle, pink fizz,
Sawdust lucky dips,
Boiled sweets in striped pyjamas,
The petal scent and fizz of sweetness.
The sherbet twists of my childhood.

The dark taste of liquorice
Purpling lips like a punch in the mouth.

Daisy-chains and Nettle-stings

Hiding in the bushes,
The smell of cap-guns,
The crack of the cap –
I want it all back.

Grubby knees, orchard trees,
Throwing pebbles, bouncing balls,
The fizz, the surprise
Of Dandelion and Burdock;

Dragonflies on the stream,
Skimmed stones, dipped toes,
Fingers trailing in the water.
The future bright as crocuses;

Dock leaves, dandelions,
Puppy dog tails and tadpole jars,
Rosehip times and sundial hours
Under the trees' pewter branches;

Gorse, broom, torn grass,
Conker fights, climbing trees
Dandelions, counting time.
Holding hopes. Yours. Mine.

Chocolate Buttons, Warm Hand Days

Milk top mornings, dry stone walls,
Measuring life by feet and inches,
Then shrinking inside to Mrs Pepperpot size
As chalk hits the blackboard,
Scratches, screams.

Playground

Skipping ropes, sports days, playground games,
Ring a ring o' roses
Ropes twist in the air,
Bright ribbons in the girls' hair.
Powder-shot brilliant sunshine.

We all fall down.

Dinner-time

Handstands in the playground,
Haggle in the yard,
Huddle away from the rain.

Let's play Poison.

Egg and Spoon

Chance, balance,
Careful progress,
Rough hessian sacks,
Three-legged rush
Stumbling forward,
Leapfrogging for freedom.

Beanstalk

The toddler on the tangled forest carpet
Climbs up the beanstalk leaves
Into the clouds' dreamy-white pages.

Promises

Hope rolls away like a marble,
The bright ribbon within the rounded glass
Winking at me
In a game I know I'll never win.

Bullet

The sweetie-jar is on the top shelf,
Just out of reach.
I want to bite the bullet.

Savour

Life's pattern was once cut out
Like the lace-paper doilies
We used on Sunday afternoons.
Cup-cakes,
Currant buns,
Sweet taste.
Crumbs.

Tuckshop

Inching up the measuring-stick,
Nag of lessons, school bell,
Youth's crispiness in my mouth,
Adventure on my tongue,
Sweet mint feathers in the breeze,
Afternoon butter-cups under my chin,
Daisy-petals.
Loves me. Loves me not.

Mint Cake

Femur-thin blades on skates
Wobbling like a bike without stabilisers.
Trying to balance
Arms out, stand tall,
Biting cold,
Rubbing hands,

Skating on thin ice.

Jigsaw

Sister and brother
Play together,
Fighting, arguing,
Sharing,
Looking for the missing
Pieces of the jigsaw.

Halcyon Liquorice

Sweet sunshine days
Staring at the sugar-cane windows.

Puppy-fat stuck to the
Black-leather seat of the car.

Holiday

The conch-shell contains the echoes
Of childhood holiday secrets,
The bouncing light.

Beached

Sand in the toes,
Kneeling childhood
Pebbles pull to time's undertow.

The tide washes everything away.

Hide and Seek

I have lost myself.
In the bedroom, through the wardrobe
Inside an enchanted, winter world
Of footprints in the snow.

Delight.

Bobbins

Tissue patters, chalk, threads,
Scissors cut the life out of the cloth,
Rolls of linen, skeins of wrapped silk,
Button boxes, thimbles, bobbins,
Pins and needles, tacks,
Pin up high, tuck, fold, judge,
Square tiles on the lino floor,
Scratched by the wear of women's heels.
Patterns, press-studs, bows,
Pattern packs, accessory racks,
The old till creaks in the dusted quietness.
High shelves hold the promise of fashions
That will never come back.

Slow Things

Swan on the water
Rippled rainbow light
Calm the leaping summer spirit
Of childhood.

Pirates

Cannon balls and shipwrecks,
Galleons on the Coral Reef,
Captain Pugwash, Seaman Staines,
Long before we knew what it all meant.

Cannon balls and shipwrecks,
Pirate ships, sails raised,
Tilting on the waves,
Prisoners walking the plank.

Cannon balls and shipwrecks,
Coral harbours, Blackbeard,
Mermaids perched on rocks,
The blue ocean waves of freedom.

Cannonball and shipwrecks
Men in tights, sword-fights
Grappling hooks and treasure.
Privateers.

Sweet Afternoons

Honey sweet afternoons are gone.
The hive attacked
The honeycomb bitter.

Hot Afternoon

Snoring in the hot afternoon,
Flies scud the river's surface;
Blossom on the tree
Hides the turquoise kingfisher
Hungry on the opposite bank.

Snow White

Snow White
Takes a bite
Of the tasty fruit of temptation.

Sudden sunset darkness,
Blood-moon cracks like an egg,
Dragon wings lift in the sky,
Diamond scales twisting in her sleep.

Birthday Parties

Cobwebbed are the chandeliers,
Hung with torn streamers
Life's wax drips,
The candle burns at both ends,
The Dandelion and Burdock has gone flat.

Tearing the newspaper,
Pass the Parcel,
Hide and Seek,
Chinese Whispers,
Blind Man's Buff.

Bathtime

Childish bubbles
Sky blue sunshine
Draining down the plug hole.

On the Shelf

The rag doll sits tired on the shelf,
Staring out of the window
At the children's tea-party
On the checked cloth on the grass.

Before

I'm going to the factory
With my golden ticket.
To taste the curling leaves of candy plants,
Squeeze wide-eyed wonder
From this treasure-trove journey:
Rivers of chocolate,
Smooth milk-brown waters,
Liquorice leaves,
Sweetness hanging in the air.

Before the gates of the factory closes
And the padlocks shut.

Rich Pickings

Rich pickings for them
And their plum private-school accents.
I want to wrestle the conversation to the ground
Teenage rage left in the rubbish
By the dustbin.

But

But secondary school has other girls,
Groups who taunt, play by other rules,
Who know how to scratch,
Put a match
To my childhood.

Creation

Eve steps from the ferns,
Tropical springs, fruit-sweet life.
Browned bite-marks, sable tears.
Her offspring with their Janus face-off
Kill the bird of paradise
With an arrow laced in venom.

They snarl, turning on each other
Under the burning sky orb.

Bounty

She is singing to the serpent
The teeth-marked core lies on the grass.
Truth and lies.
She is tempting.
If she is his heart's desire
He can't be all rotten.

Still a glimpse of good in the lad, then.

Heavenly Bite

This rosy globe of promise,
Crystalized ruby orb,
Peridot glistening,
She wants its succulent taste.

But is not as sweet as it looks,
Poisoned to the core,
It will pull her down to cinders and dry ash.

Her small paradise shrinks, closes in,
Looped by the hangman's serpent noose.
The garden darkens and weeds grow up,
Tangled, nettled,
Life flaps breathless, turning to fossils.

Everyone born changes to a curled corpse.
Everything has changed
The mirror shatters
To show the mirror image of her sons.

Expelled

There is a gate
And a padlock with no key.

On the garden wall the gargoyles hiss.

Beyond the gate there is only
A wilderness, parched and rocky underfoot.

She wears a dark veil
In a vale of tears
Wet pearls on her face.

Icarus

Feather-constructed to carry
His peacock beauty
On feathered fronds
Of filigree nets.

Limbs spanned out like a frog,
Spread eagled,
He's going to have a big impact.

Lucifer

Crashing to earth,
Trying to grasp onto the clouds and the moondust
And the exterior of the world and the heavens.
Feeling his lack of substance in his limbs and wings,

Collapse of innocence,
Black smog,
Chasm and cavern,
Buried alive.

When you swat a month
All you are left with is dust on the wall.

Tadpole Swimming Genes

Blood moon,
Savage eye,
Wolf howl,
Human cry.

Evolution

Aged, caged face,
Ravaged, savaged,
Squashed ape under the sky's turmoil,
Struggling from the boiling river,
Standing on two feet
Chewing bones,
Walking tall,
And yelling.

Flint to Flint

Fire blaze,
Spear skin,
Blood daubed walls,
Flint, fire, blade, death,
Animal roars,
Human jaws.
Hunched form,
Dipped head,
Dropped jaw,
Dipped chin,
Feral growl,
Human scowl,
Rock, stone, bronze,
Closed fists,
Clenched fists,
Rock, stone, scissors, knife.

Hunger

We all share the same skeleton,
Skimmed bone,
Honed flesh,
Hunger.

Tectonic plates shift in the blood.

Slime

The lizard slithers
Out of the river
And stands in the dirt
In an Armani shirt.

Grunting Form

Reptile mood, caveman roar,
Wild eye, dropped jaw,
Scavenging for left-overs,
Daubing blood on walls,
Club, spear,
Chase, hunt,
Crawling from the gibbering swinging times
To the grunt, grunt, grunt of the monkey bunch.

Forest

We may be born in a clearing
But we die in the forest,
Dim light closing in.

Damp Eaten

Empty draughts wrap around the walls
Corn dollies hang
In the mulled autumn light.
Cold itches round the room.

Mist, frost and frozen breath,
Fruits and colours wither and mildew,
Curl away like cold ashes in the grate
In the year's lateness.

Autumn Days

The bleak weather is here to stay.
Nagged by frost, mist, draughts,
Fogged cobblestone design,
Silver painted grass.
The hopping robin challenges the cold.
Nibbling the membrane of my mouth,
Jarring my teeth,
The weather punishes comings and goings.
Autumn offers a withered,
Weathered old handshake to Winter.

Hawthorn

Hawthorn spiked birdsong
Shatters the dawn-cream blossoms,
Breath razor-sharp.

Field

Crinkling copper bracken,
Partridge wings tremble,
Damp air, rotting leaves.

Cold Blue

Harvested pumpkins leer
In furrowed brown fields,
Indigo tipped aerials
Meet the icy skyline.

Twisted

Dying are the ornamental
Branches of the cherry tree
Boughs in agony.

Apple

Hanging fruitfulness,
A hollow skull,
Wasps gather.

Web

The butterfly struggles
In the cobweb's thimble fineness.
The spider climbs down its filmy net.

Mildewed Leaves

Spotted darkness,
Shrivelled bloom,
Dead-headed happiness.

Cold Land

Rusted signs, lost names,
Collieries, factories,
Gas works, breweries,
Teesside, Weardale, Tyneside.
Sharp corn ears
Bending to dirt earth
In the furrowed light
Of dawn's torn horizon.

Wasted

In the wasteland of growing up
Time ticks like a bomb
The tap drips.

Slowed

Bridge-bolts rust,
Arches rust,
Lost names,
Fogged panes,
Broken rails,
Seams ripped,
Tunnels bricked up,
Stations closed,
Pistons progress
Slowed.

But this town still remembers
The fire-breathing industry,
Dragon-lunged locomotives.

Always

Always the dust-pocked window,
The grind of grit, dust,
Metal riot, metal riot. Rust.

Eyes Shut

To what is being done to this town
In the name of progress,
Blowing their trumpets for a few months.

This town is like a little girl,
Curls combed, scented, all dressed up,
Who has lost her smile.

Brim

On a seat marked by aerosol paint
In an area of town that stinks of urine,
The bins are full of rubbish.

Glamour and Glee

Bored shop windows yawn wide,
Prices dreaming,
Shop dummies' modesty exposed.
Glamour and glee.

Always offering more for less.

Tomcats

Snaggletooth men on the prowl
Against the jawline of the sky,
Looking for a fight.
Caterwauling.

Batwing Thoughts

I want to see the lantern's glow,
Racoon faces seeking traces of buttercup light from the surface,
Valley field greenness above,
Veins of mineral hope below,
Coal flakes, dust motes hanging in the air
In tunnels, shafts, narrow gaps, under the earth
Before the pits were closed down,
Beneath meadow ghost-flowers
Before the shops were shuttered,
The club shut
And the glum terraces closed their eyes.

Gleam

The belligerent voices
Demanding their rights
Are silent
Their buried skeletons forgotten
Their patched and marching banners
Held high, taut, bright in the museum.

The trail of industry's hot breath,
The drag of steam,
Whistle of wind
Time's lost progress
Confined, consigned to a shiny museum.

Nearly

Spikes on the heart monitor.
The hospital is slowly closing down.
This town is nearly dead.

Angel

Got to find me an angel,
Got to find me an angel,
Before my vision cracks.
Got to find me an angel,
Before my heart and lips crack.

Got to find me an angel,
Before this distress
Takes my heart, this black brick
This thin blackness.

Got to find me an angel
To calm my heart.

Fall

Rosebay Willowherb,
Buttercup meadow,
Tall feathered grass.

The scythe swings in an arc,
Cuts me down at the knees.

Woodpecker

Leaves are carried away by the wind,
The woodpecker pounds out a list of names
Tattooed in bark.

Caged

Sunflower seeds,
Beady brown eye,
Inquisitive sniff,
Bored and tired
Of staring in the mirror
And going round and round
On the hamster wheel.

Song

The nightingale that sang
On hope's high branches
Has lost its song.

Decay

Fruit-flies and wasps
Swarm and flit and buzz like black locust dots
On the flesh of a brown apple-core
Thrown away in the grass.

A bitter fruit
That tastes of lizard-acid.

Words

Tearing off a scab
Until
It bleeds.

Away

Hanging over the bridge,
Sailing paper boats,
Time floats away from me.

Taxed

Time taxed
I carry these weary sacks,
Set a match to the worthless bonfire
Of my life.

Struggling

I want to be something else:
A pool of mercury, changing liquid shape,
A soap bubble of childish magic,
An apple bitten to the core.

I long to be a butterfly
But time pins down my struggling wings.

Dandelion

The dandelion roars
Then goes back to sleep,
Dreaming of pavements split
By yellow maned weeds.

Puzzle

I was the wrong bit of the jigsaw,
In the background, unseen,
Lost in the bigger picture.

I Want

I want the day back, the copper brushing leaves of light
The crunch and whisper of the grass,
The green damp sunlight.

Age

I am an ammonite,
Curling into a fossil
In the caverns of lost happiness.

Show Off

Strutting glamour
Rainbow filigree,
Shrill voice.

The peacock feather stares back at me.

Distrust

Spreads
Thick and sweet
As marmalade.

Speechless

Age finds its throat
Clogged
With lost feelings.

Autumn

Chinese lanterns,
Curled grass,
Worn earth,
Daylight dims.
I wait for something to change.

Rogue

Roaming elephants of anger and intolerance
Stampede in the wilderness.

Washing-up

I hate the draining-board,
The way it waits for you to wash-up.

I hate the washing-up,
The mugs, the cups, the suddy water.

How

Seconds tick past
With the flecked seeds of weeds in the breeze.
Dead nettles flower in the cracked pavements.
How do I hold back the years
On this soot-black turf?

Chilled

We live in deeds, not years,
In feelings, not in time.
The grass stirs,
In the lichened-chalked church-yard
Swayed dandelions bow their heads.

We live in deeds, not years,
Not in figures on the dial,
But through touch and memory.
We wander through the mist,
Cherished and chilled.
Bone-cold roads glisten with ice,
Colours wither and mildew
Like ashes in the grate.

Dog Eat Dog

Life barks,
Snarls
And bites back.

Jackpot

Flashing lights and dirty carpets,
A handful of coins warming in my tight fist,
I touch the buttons,
Kick the machine.
And wait for my winnings.

Rage

They slam the book shut
So they don't have to see
Anything that doesn't agree
With their idea of perfection.

Ready

In the attic elderly toys
Still wait to be played with,
Action Man, still dressed in khaki,
Muscled, waiting
To grab life by the throat.

Rapunzel

Roses grow up to my window
Through the thorns and thistles
That clamour around me.

Unlike

The dog is dying of melancholy.
The cat has escaped.
Unlike me.

Secrets

Promises kept, tears wept,
Summer floats away
Like dandelion seeds.

Too

Life is a tightrope
Too narrow
To walk wearing a blindfold.

Fragile

Flames flicker among the ash in the grate
I put the needle to the thread,
Sew up the remnants.

Baking

I sit at the worn, wood, flour-dusted table
And look out of the window.
The pastry is cut – bursting open with taste,
Scales tip, dip,
Weighed dough, pricked and risen
Pastry kneaded, sugar-leaved,
Cut into warm pieces;
The sieve shivers with powder
Over the spiced-cake,
The almond is smoothed.

Then time reduces everything to crumbs.